Polishing
The Bayonet

First Edition # 661   of 1000

Polishing The Bayonet

Elisabeth A. Belile

INCOMMUNICADO PRESS

P.O.BOX 99090, SAN DIEGO CA 92169 USA

Contents

Forewarning

Polishing the Bayonet acknowledges that though the pen is mightier than the sword, it can't hurt to carry one.

My favorite thing in the world is to SPEAK my poetry. To become a vessel for the voice to come through. Sound produces karma, and the human voice conveys pure emotion and therefore conveys the truth...or a lie. Give me beauty! Give me sex! Give me love and death! Ecstasy and terror! Chaos and human error! Give me lovers of men, haters of misogyny! Castrating bitches and mommies! Racist alcoholics and gangsters! Give it to me STRAIGHT. I can take it. I NEED it! Oh, and...make it *funny*.

I live in Los Angeles. I came here to write for TV. I write and produce CD ROM for a living. I am interested in writing for visual mass media. I was born a poet. It's my native tongue. I love it and I don't know why. I watch TV and movies, and I READ. A lot. I listen to music every day, all kinds of music. I play guitar and sing.

Since I moved to LA we've had rioting and uprising in the streets...floods...fire...earthquakes...a Republican mayor. God hates Los Angeles. It's a hard place to be a warrior, but man, you just GOTTA be.

I'm angry at the way "our generation" is portrayed in the news. HEY! There *are* some of us out here who spend as much time developing our brains and our weird job skills as the baby boomers spend developing stock options or "bad" neighborhoods. We are just as literate in pop culture as we are in Proust. We have that option, and it's not like we have to choose between Lucy Ricardo and Lucy Lippard...we can have it ALL! Madonna AND the Mona Lisa.

Imagine that we finally have at our fingertips the ability to go back and correct the history books. Malcolm was murdered, but his autobiography became a hot seller again when the movie came out. The same is true of Virginia Woolf's *Orlando.* Which is not to say that the book (any book) needs to be made into a movie to reach the next generation. But sometimes it helps. The stories of our culture, the history and the tribal dream songs, etc., will be remembered...*by any means necessary.*

I like to use a combination of collage, cut-up, and computer spellcheck. The collage often consists of phrases I pick up from eavesdropping, conversation, the radio, women's magazines, plagiarizing my friends' work, or paraphrasing found literature. The title poem is an epic encompassing all of my favorite themes: the war on women, racism, sexual politics, disease, dreaming, genealogy, living here, loving here, unleashing the killer inside me to write. Birth through fire.

Much of this book came from my MFA days at Naropa. A chronicle of my twenties. Rock n Roll, drugs, booze, road trips, crazy love affairs, desperation and transcendence. The Jack Kerouac School of Disembodied Poetics. Trying to be an activist, an archivist, poetic living and ways of seeing. Inspiration comes from all sources.

I would like to acknowledge, in no particular order, a few people who have changed my life and greatly influenced this work, whether they realize it or not...Beth Borrus, Linda J.

Albertano, Lisa Campbell, Anne Waldman, Merilene M. Murphy, Joan Valencia, Jack Brewer, Eleni Sikelianos, Angela B. Coon, Kimi Sugioka, Cornelia Hansen, Allen Ginsberg, Harvey R. Kubernik, Katie Yates, Ivan Suvanjieff, Tom Peters, Weba Garretson, Chris Funkhouser, Bobbie Louise Hawkins, Hakim Bey, Clint Frakes, Jack Collom, the late, great Harry Smith, and many, many others out there. Thanks.

I would also like to thank Gary Hustwit for wisdom and support, Christian Hoffman, and Incommunicado sisters Pleasant, Iris, and Nicole.

How many feminists does it take to screw in a light bulb?
Just ME, baby. Just me.

E.A. Belile, Los Angeles, 1994

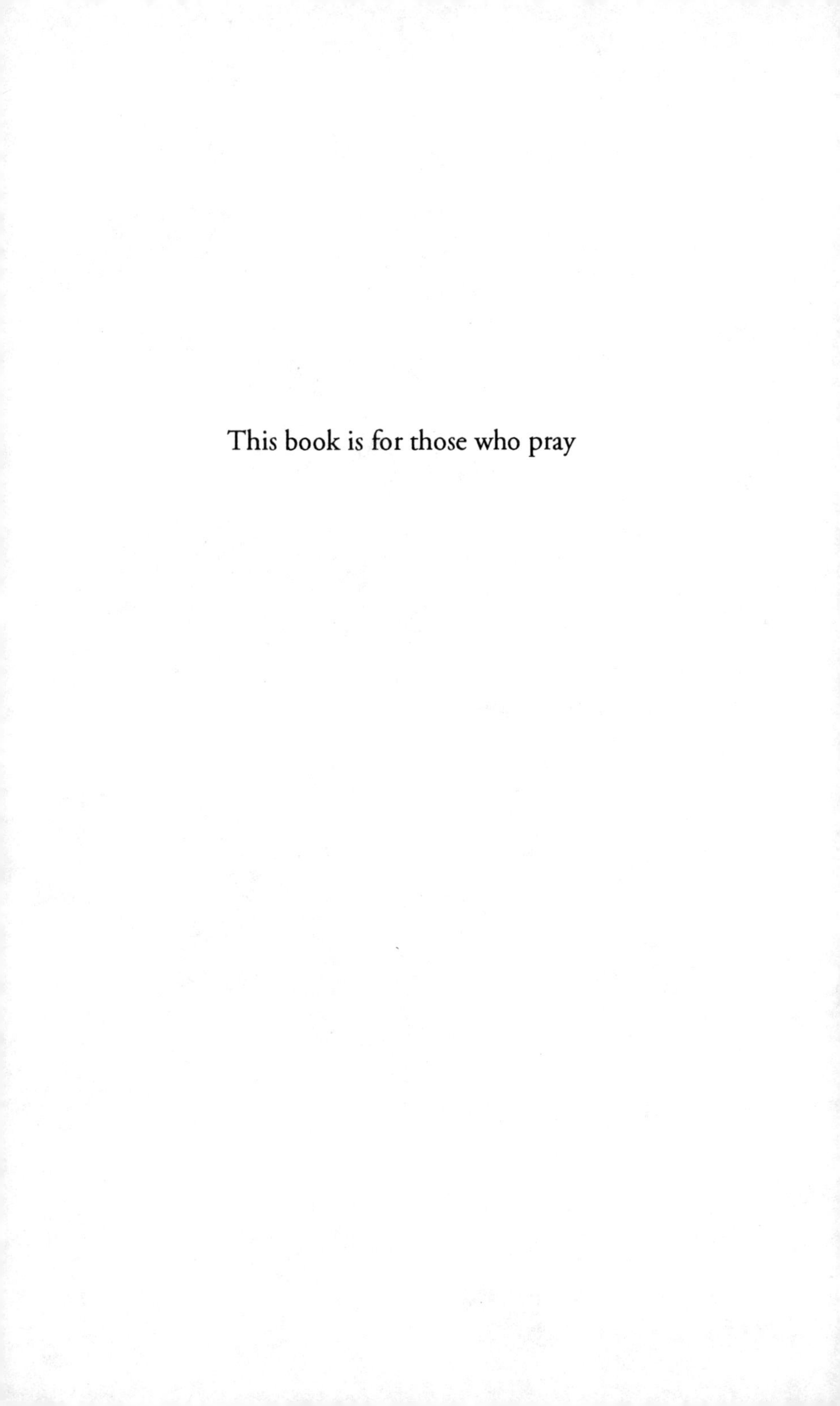

This book is for those who pray

Do I Look Fat In This?

Where were you when the bomb dropped,
weak in your knees in prayer?
Your precious cells get
pulverized
and die a little.
I debase myself for you.

Objects d'Art
—a collaboration with Beth Borrus

Eyeball. Soul Crusher. Long hair and no ass. Dark walls and no windows. All I wanted to do was get out of there alive. No one here does. I just go to Denver and die. There's some weird gentlemen here. All in preparation for Halloween. They even got an x-ray going. There is a lot of turnover, though. Where do they go?

Not to bars like this one. Black latex paint all OVER the place. The true test is NOT passing the bar. Passion oozes. Not on me. It'll cost you a quarter to re-enter. As daddy says, "there ain't no free lunch."

But I've been fairly fed. Platters splatter the walls. Vinyl rainbow. Viscous discs. The band needs some assistance. What's that burning smell? A pipe in the ashtray. This is my favorite Dick. Kill from the heart. Joey Ramone — is he here? No, no, he's ice skating in the garden, Madison Square. Power pop thrill seeker Joey cuts it all up. He's cold. Yeh, yeh.

Yeh, yeh, blondes and band members. Umm, wanna push that little black miniskirt right up over those thighs, right on over her little hill of a belly. This is what, the Big Boys?

This is the breakfast of black and white photographers. Some tye-dye black boots combination. The poetess and the boy with the long blonde whatever. In color. Let's eat. Check out the blacked out bill of fare. Secret delicacies hidden behind duct tape. You can't be a band if you don't have any duct tape. You can't have any meat. And she's a vegetarian.

This is the Big Boys on tape — sound on sound — I can't get over it. Love is high. Love is leaf-like. Wilting in living color. This is called "falling" by some people standing up. I could've stood you up but I didn't. A broomstick up your skirt. A smart witch. Glittery red platforms. Surrender in the sky. The book always rules out the movie. The sky goes metal.

Paradise lost to a parking lot. By this, I might mean California. She/had to leave. Bloody red eyesore. Sleep all night in your kitchen, or in a drunk driving car. All the bodies.

Yawn in, blow tobacco smoke out. All the best boys are taken. This is a city too easy to understand. My back aches, my neck turns. All the best ones are gone. At least this song. I know everyone here. Let's get on with it over with. Is there anything to look at? Too many tattoos. Nice rhythm for so much skinny.

But I don't know if I used the boys or the girls. "We don't care if people dance or not, as long as it's not in a circle." Speaking of circles, this guy's posture is straight from the womb. A snake keeps eating itself. An eyeball bulges out of old blue jeans. His spine is a line, I rhyme.

Even the soundman is a woman. Brutal with that mixer.

Anyway, I can remember his fingers on my face...forget it. Yeh, his mouth and my collarbone...hey! It's dark down here! The basement of my dreams. I don't wanna go. Johnny's there. Mixin' up the medicine. I always called him Roger, I can't even remember his real name anymore. One of the Real Kids. We could quit.

This is as good as it gets.

Post Master's Blues
or, Why Do I Keep Falling For Male Men?

This is where time begins. How plain women attract men. Tired of being in love with the hero, the tragic heroine narrows her eyes, rubs her hands together, and spits. Certain Jewish religious customs encourage such behavior.

All of this is true.

Harry had an entire box of fortunes from cookies. Our heroine hasn't unpacked anything since she moved that once. A roomful of furniture for two. They were everyone's favorite couple, and she was the star.

She was in love with the instructor, but Grace wanted to play. I was a fish in her catch-and-release program. Please don't tell them where she's gone. And don't wait with the light on.

Grace drove to California with her father. She believes that women don't really have a choice in travelling alone. Sometimes we live in the country, sometimes in town. On the ocean. Lately we fall in and drown. She's going to live where others go for vacation.

It ended, as all things must. Too good to be true, this happened fast. He sandblasted her name off his tower.

Something Under Thirty

This one's for Grace.

"It's a bikini world, it's a dog's life. I didn't start the beauty contest, but I can't ignore it either."
— Beth Borrus

I'm a whole-piece-suit kinda girl. Curves and a slow car. Careful. Safe. She's smart and talented too, a good mime. Shiny white teeth and eyes.

I want world peace. Sorry, I can't make it tonight – I've got to glue my angel down. It's true that the kitty likes being beaten.

Her strongest poems do not speak of love. They speak of war. So we believe.

A deserter getting stoned on synthetic heroin in the desert. Took one look and forgot all about Alexandria, about the boots and operating heavy machinery. Heavy machinery, a heart stops beating in sleep. Depressed breathing.

In love or war, hearts will attack.

I waited in bed for the phone, depressed. Breathing. Woke up to phone numbers pounding in my head. Repeating symphonies for the devil. Sure I'd fuck a fat guy. I must cease this fantasy. Turn to something real. Something fast. Something under thirty.

They all become one. One long line. Ivory smooth, tattooed a bowl of chili on his shoulder. Grew a soul patch. He's lost more weight. Skips breakfast. Started up that nasty drug habit again. "Consider me your first casualty," I said. I remember he had cancer. We sat in the doctor's office, ex-Catholics praying.

What to do before you die? Destroy Helen of Troy, Beth. Someone has given you your first gun.

I have t-shirts that adults aren't supposed to wear. White vinyl boots. Independent style music, the lite rock of tomorrow. Dear God.

"I was asked how I'd like to be remembered. I'd just like to be remembered. How could a person die and no one would know she had left the earth? No one. I'd hate to think that no one would remember me."

Youth culture lies. Focus on Rimbaud, a girl's flat belly.

When these cosmic questions get asked, I answer: "So what?" I was feeling like a mummy on the table, like my mommy on the table giving birth. But I was giving death.

Someone needs to sit that girl down
and ask her if she understands heavy metal.

Other Women

Other women look better in clothes than I do. Other women have accessories that I don't have. Mexican earrings, black flannel tights, flowered scarves, leather jackets, sporty watches. Other women have narrow thighs and funky old cars.

Every man I have ever loved has been in love with an anorexic woman.

Then there was Jan, who won a full scholarship to Yale Law School but quit to become a journalist. Jan, who now writes for NME. My boyfriend who had been obsessed with her for six years said they kissed once the entire time.

Then there was little Mary Sunshine on his wall. She was bulimic. She'd eat apple pies and vanilla ice cream and cherry cobbler and Hershey's kisses and then...she'd just get rid of it. One look at her blonde, blue-eyed, dimpled face and I thought what her parents must have thought: "What's a nice girl like *that* doing with a boy like *this*?"

Oh, how strange to receive letters from his new girlfriend — the one who sings, plays guitar, piano AND accordion. Oh how satisfied I am with her misspellings!

Other women lead more glamorous lives than I do. Other women sleep with the lead guitarist. Other women have been to Europe.

Other women live in studios and lofts with their sexy, beautiful, talented, rich, famous, artistic, creative, passionate, hilarious lovers who are *completely* obsessed with them.

"I was in love with an anorexic," many men have told me.

In the 16th century, nuns would starve themselves to get closer to God. Goodbye, evil flesh. And the sins of. There was no wine to drink, no peyote, no LSD, no sex — oh, to be the bride of Christ was enough! Goodbye, evil flesh. The high of the fast, impaled on spires, nuns die in ecstasy and no eating. Just the body and blood of you-know-who.

Eating disfigures. My orders are to hate fat.

"I have to admit that I've never made love to a woman with breasts before."

"She was so small, it was a surprise to see that she *had* breasts!"

"I used to prefer women with bodies like twelve year old boys."

When I was a twelve year old girl I prayed not to start until I was at least thirteen. When I did I was petrified. I cried, I was jealous of all the little girls who could still play and be free. I had to sit on the riverbank while the other girls got to swim in the river. I did not want to be a woman. I did not want to grow a baby inside me. It mortified me.

Then there was the morning I pretended to be asleep while he started jerking off. Who was he thinking of? Was it the high school senior from last summer, whose father sat across the breakfast table with "love" and "hate" tattooed across each set of knuckles? Or was it the one in East Africa? She was teaching

South African refugees how to read and write their own language (her third or fourth) so they could return to their country. And of course she went to Harvard — at sixteen.

Other women go to Ivy league colleges when they are adolescents. Other women are dancers. Other women are taken to the airport and longed for. Other women speak a multitude of languages. Other women will give head.

"You're wonderful, Liz. You're just too...*intense.*"

Other women do not throw dishes like I do.

Then there was Sarah, also anorexic. Wanted to be Patti Smith. And Lex, who *was* Patti Smith. She played the electric guitar amazingly well when she was fourteen. She used to blow 'em away at CBGB'S and the Mudd Club. Lex, who can rack pool balls with her arms. Lex, who rides a Harley but is also very petite and has long red hair. Wears leather all the time. I reminded him of Sarah from my forehead up.

From my forehead down I am attached to my body, which once went through a vicious Edie Sedgwick phase. I wanted ribs.

It's my eating disorder again. Eleni says when she needs to take up more space, she does. We become part of the castle. We are sisters under the skin, and bones. Some's bones are more prominent than others. Closer to skeletal.

Other women are inside me. I want to give birth to something. Other women have narrow feet, will not drink water from the bathroom sink. Other women have heard my name one too many times.

Thesis Girl
—a suggestion of Lee Ann Brown

She is that center.
She did give this title.
She's a red dress devil doll,
crowbar to the heart.
Torn under the ribs.

Villanelles for her sister,
and crying at the movies.
I remember them singing
Amazing Grace.

"Thinking is daily living," she said,
standing on bricks in front of people.

She studies with the wife of speed,
has a library tan.
Books for a face.
Nancy Drew mysteries, always
pleasant and dark.

Hiroshima, my love.
North Carolina, darling one.
New York City, my amour.

Crowbar to the skull.

"O Lake, " she said, swimming in it.
Chilled.

Thin lexicon under her skirt, a bunch of
figures in braille.

Venus de Milo.
Love and Civilization.
She is that subject.
She knows it.
All of her life.

The slip in the top drawer is filigree,
writhes at her touch.

Where the center is,
she spins to it.
It goes whap whap whap,
like a scarf caught in the propeller,
like an angel drowning in that same iced lake,
pulled as ever to the midst of it,
the deep drain.

Theme woman.

Little Sister

I see her about once a year, for Christmas. It's like always having a little kid around. Santa Claus and toys. People ask how brain-damaged she is, and I tell them that she can't dress herself, can't take a bath alone because she might have a seizure and drown, can barely write her name.

I used to wonder what retarded people dreamed about.

My uncle has a theory that Shanna is retarded because she was involved in cloning experimentation in Atlantis in one of her past lives. Apparently she was a brilliant scientist who pioneered the genetic blending of humans with animals, enslaving them. This is where minotaurs and mermaids came from. My mom and brother and I were also scientists, her close friends. And we promised her that we would come back with her, to make things a little easier when she had to live out the karma she had earned.

It would make sense that she and my brother, who are twins, came into the world together, but that there's nothing wrong with him.

I tried psychic experiments with my sister all the time. Like once we were sitting in front of the TV watching cartoons and I looked over at her and thought "If you can hear me, look at me." And she turned her face away from the screen and looked at me.

I continue to harbor this fantasy.

Last year's Christmas visit, my sister stepped out of mom's shower and slipped. She nearly bit her tongue in half when her jaw caught the enamel edge of the tub. She started crying, began convulsing, and my mom clung to her helplessly. I rushed in and helped pull Shanna to her feet. She was hunched over and whimpering, bleeding hard and still seizing. We walked her to the bed and put her in it. My mom left the room to go clean up the blood, and I bent over Shanna, who was still shaking and sobbing. I put my hands over her head and I closed my eyes, feeling the heat emanating from my palms and soaking into Shanna's skull, into her brain.

"Stop it," I commanded silently. Her breath caught and her eyes flew open at the same time mine did. "Stop it," I whispered, staring into their green depths. She stopped shaking and started to shiver, and swallowed like a very sleepy child. I smiled deeply into her face. "Stop it," I said again. She half giggled, blinked, and sighed, then ceased all spasming completely. "Enough." My own tears dropping on her cheeks. I kissed her forehead and she laughed, then drifted off to sleep.

I told my father this story, and he said, "You know, I had a strange incident with Shanna many years ago. She must have been eight or nine. I was lying on my back in the middle of the floor in the living room, doing some visualizing or meditation..."

At one point during the seventies my father was really into pyramid power. I remember he'd come home all excited that the dull razor blades he'd placed under his friend's home pyramid were sharp again. Also, he kept fresh fruit from rotting for months at a time by sticking them under the pyramid.

"Shanna walked in and laid down right across from me, her head touching mine, with her arms and feet spread out like mine. It was weird. But then I started to visualize myself going over to her, and I imagined myself reaching in and scooping out her brain to cleanse it, when all of a sudden she just sat right up and said, 'it's okay, daddy, it's okay.' Then she patted my arm and got up and left."

Weird.

I go to my great-grandmother's old house, and she is cooking rice and gravy at the stove. I walk in and she turns to face me. Her eyes are extraordinarily bright and her mouth is extraordinarily large; she has on shocking pink lipstick that looks like she tried to put it on in a big hurry so that it's outside the lines a little. She speaks to me, calls me "Chere" like she always did, but her lips aren't moving. I look into the bedroom. It still has that mothball smell and the top half of the Sacred Heart of Jesus statue over the bed.

My sister is sitting there, smiling, and she floats toward me. Tells me, telepathically, that everything is ok and that we can communicate in this way. I'm afraid because I know that my great grandmother is dead now, but my sister just laughs and makes me feel better.

Helen

I.

Helen works for the Salvation Army, and she was coming by the studio to pick up some tapes they had made for a training film. *Did you know that the Southland Corporation, which owns 7-11, also owns the Salvation Army?* Well, anyway, she's a real nice woman (*straight blonde hair held back with pins, steely grey strands loose/pale ponds creams face/upper lip twitching/mosquito/ she listens*) she must be a little older than me, in her later fifties, you know I'm at the golden years, young old age — doesn't it feel strange? I remember my own parents beginning to look old (*yes I remember the beautiful dark laugh lines still laughing in repose/big round gypsy mama/baubled necklaces dripping down the front of her/loose robes and black hair/deep, expensive perfume smell, always/jet black curls/one yellowed tooth up front in a mouth that rarely smiled then*) boy was that rough. Well Helen is just as nice as can be, and she thought all these years that she couldn't have children have I reminded you that I want grandchildren? Don't do anything foolish now, but soon. Did you know that Missy is pregnant again? And she's not sure who the father is? She and LaDeen, both pregnant and smoking! Can you believe it? Who's LaDeen? Wilton's wife. Pretty little girl. (*when I was eighteen/brought Richard a bag of oranges for his cold/rocked in a boy's arms for the first time/drank gin and tonics, dancing til four/ studied just enough to pass a physics final*) Anyway, Helen thought she couldn't have children all this time, then she got pregnant when she was forty four, it just came as a surprise, and she gave birth to Michael. And she is crazy about that boy.

Did you know, when she was on the delivery table, his heart stopped beating — you know, they have those fetal heart monitors for riskier births, like when the mother is older — his heart stopped beating, and the doctors told her that they had to perform a Cesarean right there on the spot, but that they wouldn't have time to use an anesthetic... (what?) so they asked her if they could just cut her open right there without it, to save the baby's life, and she said yes.

She said the pain was excruciating

like bones being crushed

Helen smiles her attractive woman smile and says
"Every day I thank God for him."

She said the pain was excruciating.

Have you ever seen a Cesarean birth? It's strange — the baby comes out all pink and dry *(Image of white powder, like packing, lifting)* and it's quite peaceful.

"Everyday I thank God for him."

II.

Momma.
Ma mere.
L'amour.
The sea.

"Can I have the keys tonight?"

A gentle lurching inside her when he leaves.

When his heart stops beating/
I'll know.

What fabric tears away,
this
fragile
moss-like
veins of love
and green
when his
heart
will

cease.

Crazy Minerva

(dr. john bongos under whispers)

Crazy Minerva
cast her spell across the table,
we closed a drawer which said
she was crazy.

I believe in good and evil.

So what.

Crazy Minerva
was truly Cleopatra
blackness dominating from her eyes.

I believe in good and evil.

Crazy Minerva
spilled her blood in the Sahara
Janis Joplin was murdered by the press.

I believe in good and evil.

so what.

Pussy

You say/ when you heard me say the word
"cunnilingus"
your mouth turned to water

I was there in my brown eyelet dress

I was whispering

"cunnilingus"

and your lips
your mouth
was

your green eyes
your long black hair

it is nirvana, you say/
milk and honey, you say/
nectar of the goddess, you say/
manna, you say/

lick your lips your mouth is
ever so
slightly open,
panting a little

your breath is warm

I love it, you say/
lifting your eyes

moving your lips
slow

I love to eat
to drink

you want to lick, you say/
you want to put those lips
that tongue

you are vibrating
I am almost naked

you put those lips that/
hot breath
against the/elastic waistband of my
white
cotton
panties

my hips are still,
coiled
can't believe how good/
waiting

your leg is wet from me
sliding/your thigh

then

your hot breath
on that hipbone
that little tendon that
little tender tendon between
my pussy lips and my thigh
that
sweet puffy place that
tight tendon
you spread my legs you slip those panties
clean
off

you put your whole face inside my pussy.

Oh it tastes sweet, you say/

you come up for air

my nipples are hard
as my fingertips,
your fingers
sliding in and out of my cunt oh

one

two

three

three

four of your
fingers dripping,

dippin' in
and out/
of my cunt

oh

my hips are uncontrollable now
an undulating stealth

inside
how I wish those four
fingers
inside my pussy/were

your cock

your tongue full on my clit
you make it small and spicy, ticklish

my clit your teeth
smooth under soaking lips.

The smell is incredible, you say/
breathing

your whole body
is in it

my whole body
arched
for your lips
tongue
teeth

working in and out and
along my swelling clit.

There is an ocean of manna flowing,
a river of nectar,
a symphony
a moaning from outside of my body

you turn me over.

My legs are like candy, you say/
biting into them
my ass is gorgeous, you say/
cupping it under your hand

you spread my ass cheeks
my head hangs over the bed

you probe for my cunt,
we slide over each other
your mouth
sucking
my pussy

I am shivering.

I want you inside so bad
you keep
licking and
sucking
and my heart
is beating

my heart is
beating

my heart
pumping
and
pumping

my heart
in my
belly
comes

forth

Val Young

Val Young was afraid of being possessed by the devil. She would break into a sweat, hyperventilating and counting out crazy rhythm tracks in her head. She had to quit playing her instruments, clarinet and guitar. The beat induced the fear attacks. She would grip the edges of her chair during Algebra and swoon.

In Haiti, it is an honor if certain gods possess you.

Sometimes she would test herself by dredging up someone's name from high school, or earlier, and if she couldn't remember the last name, she would go through the entire alphabet until she hit it. People so often physically resembled their names.

Rhonda Rossi. Jerry Hoose. Peggy Rose. Berta Cossey. Brad White. Tammy Ubanoski.

It was eerie.

When her mother tried to explain the theory of relativity, she said to "imagine as if past, present, and future were all contained in one, indeterminable moment." Val grasped the notion immediately. That song came on the radio: "Baby, I'm yours...and I'll be yours...until two and two is three...yours...until the mountains crumble to the sea."

She began to research dreaming.

Kristin's twin sister, who had died at birth, woke Val up from a deep sleep. Val was confused. They went and stood on Interstate 10, on the west side of the Lake Charles bridge, waiting for a school bus to come for them. Once they had reached the middle of the bridge she could see a small group of people standing on the shore below, waving. "Who are they?" she wondered.

"They are the dead."

Val was alive, but she had the ability to communicate with the dead, and they were eager to speak to her. The sister told her that everything was ok.

She was, and probably always will be, afraid of the devil.

Specific epiphanies and symbolic dreams stand out. Val's stunning psychedelic epiphany, which she felt the first time she took mushrooms, occurred to her while crawling around on her hands and knees in a vacant lot: "Wow! Everything is *really* stupid!"

She spent a lot of time obsessively dividing all phrases into "threes." Counting each letter, punctuation mark, contractions, etc., and manipulating them to the point until they worked. Like:

"Baby, I'm yours...and I'll be yours...until two and two is three...yours...until the mountains crumble to the sea."

Could be divided into:

"Bab yI' myo urs...and I'l lbe you rsu nti ltw oan dtw ois thr eey...our sun til the mou nta ins cru mbl eto the sea."

Val was terrified of developing stigmata.

When she was about twelve years old, she healed a paper cut just by staring at it. She hyperventilated, ran downstairs, and stood in the kitchen shaking. Her mother came down and gave her a tranquilizer.

Did people in restaurants vaguely suspect that Val was famous?

It wasn't so much the devil anymore, not since Val had studied ESP and Haitian voodoo possession. It was people who died and wanted to connect with her, due to her honed psychic abilities.

Once she asked the Ouija board if she had ever been anyone famous. It said "Yes." And when she asked who, it said "Jean Harlow." So she went to the library and studied books on Jean Harlow. Years later, when she visited the old MGM lot in Culver City, she tried desperately to remember it. "Turn here," she would say authoritatively.

Why didn't more of her friends want to take pictures of her?

It wasn't so much the devil anymore.

Convinced that she would eventually die of a fatal disease, Val glanced at her weak, short lifeline, thinking that it got longer every time she quit drinking coffee.

Val was terrified of spontaneously combusting.

She worries about the bomb that went off in San Antonio when her mom was pregnant for her.

Val really enjoys male homoerotica.

On video, two women dressed head to toe in latex bondage gear are writhing on screen together. The countess in *Lair of the White Worm*. One woman stands over the other, dripping manna from her vagina into the other's open mouth.

It's not so much the devil anymore.

Breaking the Idol

"You're treading on the virgin!"
You're re-naming the street
you have built condos over burial grounds,
you

Crash's Gash

Used to you could fuck.

Someone had to take the blame; looks like the prostitutes were being fingered for this crime.

Crash was coming down. Hard. One more clink of silver and she'd move that sequined bikini strap over and start stroking her clit, in full view. That oughtta perk up his pecker.

Marina with her rabbit teeth and her black half moon eyes. Angular, huge hands and shoulder blades. She tells Crash in her breathless voice: "I dreamed about the theater last night, the one you always dream about with Lee. I saw it! And Lee was there."

Through a haze of methamphetamine, and moisture pellets from heavy breathing, and cigarette tar residue gathering on the glass, Crash could see that this guy was definitely an "empty" one. She sighed. Christ.

"The thing about Marina is, she was born sad."

They'd usually watch until you got to fingerfucking yourself, maybe once in a while with a toy, while they'd be staring off into X-ray land, dreaming about their wives or their daughters or ramming their uncovered cocks repeatedly into the cunt of an exaggeratedly ecstatic stranger, and you'd be wildly hammering your pointy finger, then your "the finger" finger, then your ring finger in what you hoped was your soaking wet pussy, and maybe they'd jerk off with you and then leave. If you were lucky. Crash's head was starting to split open. God, she hoped she was lucky.

Sitting on Ray's bed, watching him tighten the belt around his arm with his teeth. Watching him plunge the needleful of speed in, tightening his jaw in ecstasy, his eyes changing to white. And then he'd pass the needle to Mohawk Scott, and Billy Faggot. Billy's black curly head. His black market Marxist literature. He believed in that shit. Dead Billy.

The amph had heightened Crash's senses so that every smell in the place tore current-like into her stomach.

She belched a dry one. Unhh, the stench was unbearable. She broke into a cold sweat. Could feel her body temperature dropping as the waves of nausea began.

Grace insists that they do another line of speed. Crash is sharply aware of the fullness of Grace's mouth, the deep lines, the sinewy skin and cream color hair. "You're the pretty one, " Grace tells her. Crash silently disagrees, says aloud, "You just can't handle the fact that you're sexy." They drink more beer, not yet cold enough, but what the fuck.

A small roomful of people sit mesmerized by bootleg Rocky and Bullwinkle cartoons. Blue and white flickering strobes light their faces from underneath. The band who lives here plays a jangly guitar disc in the next room. People are dancing. Grace lays out another line of speed with a razor blade. She calls out to Crash. Crash is dry humping a tall, homely rock critic in the dark against the hallway wall while they are waiting to pee. Grace strolls over, casually rolls the critic off of Crash, and grabs her breasts fiercely, with passion. He slumps to the floor and pisses himself. Grace forces her tongue into Crash's mouth, they step over him. The bathroom door opens. A guy with long dark lank hair in a Grateful Dead tie dye t-shirt mumbles an apology and stumbles into the Rocky and Bullwinkle room. Crash pulls Grace into the bathroom with her. Grace stops. "I'm scared." "So am I," Crash says, throwing her to the floor and kicking the door shut.

Most of the girls had quit using amph on the job after the first month or so. Not Crash. She was a glutton for anything that brought you closer to enlightenment, and she had tried everything.

Meditation, goddess worship, holotropic breathing, corsets, peyote, piercing, Sufism, alchemy, starvation, prostration, B&D, you name it. So when this new brand of drug hit the streets, she was ripe for it. It was supposed to be the short cut, the opening of all the right primordial memories. How to remember the genetic code of your ancestors. Of course there were possible side effects. And mutinies.

One girl got claustrophobic in her box, spun out, broke through all the glass screaming, exploding, and cut herself and the client to shreds. She bled to death in the row while the other girls flipped out, banging on the glass while the guardians vanished from the scene. Crash had never seen more giz in her life. Or more blood.

That thought, combined with screeching decibels of white hot sound pounding inside her, made Crash puke. She hadn't eaten in days, of course, so it was more like heaving foam — spewing wet white globules all over her glistening, nearly naked body. Uncooked egg whites flowing over oil. She was lying on her back with her thighs spread, opening up a full view of her cunt to the person sitting on the other side of the glass.

"This is it. I'm really dying this time," she groaned.

Her finger came to a dead halt against her clit, her head and shoulders dropped to her chest, white drool bled out of her mouth. A man wearing a helmet with bull horns and a bull's face comes thundering up on a dark horse, wielding a sword. She has one second to catch his enraged eyes before he brings the sword down on her left shoulder and cuts through her robes, her body. The sensation of her breasts falling, hitting hard ground, dust. Her hips and legs toppling onto her. Even the thought, that he had been wearing the uniform of her army.

Crash heard the old familiar swish of the glass lifting, felt the cool quickness of the membrane enveloping her body and melting into it. Then he was on top of her. He must have slipped extra coins into the slot. Crash recoiled in disgust. A puke freak. She'd heard of them. Intellectually, it made sense. After all, the days when you could actually *safely* experience firsthand another person's secretions were long gone.

Tears, piss, shit, come — it made Crash shudder, even in her near-death state.

He was all over her, gasping, grabbing her around the neck, frantically licking her breasts, belly, mouth — trying to taste the vomit. "Oh, please," he moaned. His wilted dick had become a throbbing hard-on. Crash almost laughed, which made her puke again. She marveled at the membrane, so technically advanced. It was designed to adhere to the body like a second skin the minute it got wet. It was a miracle substance, non-toxic, which had never been known to tear or slip. The membrane had made sex possible again. At least some form of sex.

He was groaning in ecstasy, the membrane so thin he could actually run his tongue along the lines of Crash's body and move the globs of vomit around, smearing her with it. He shoved his cock into her and she lifted her hips to meet his as he began pumping.

Crash couldn't believe she'd gotten a puke freak. It was kind of wild. She'd done a couple of blood freaks, reaching seductively for the scalpel, among her many tools, and carefully cutting a fine line across her collarbone. Usually the guys would shake their heads "no," and she would move on to another tactic. But the blood freaks would nod vigorously, and get visibly even hotter as she sliced. They definitely came the fastest. And blood freaks were definitely common.

The guy came in short, hot spurts. The membrane did not de-sensitive you to temperature. Crash gasped in overwhelmed, post-coital, speed hangover relief. The puke freak was heavy on top of her. She could smell the beer in his sweat, see the stubble on the back of his neck. This guy was heading for heart attack city. Probably ate hormone soaked beef, too.

She could feel his penis still vibrating inside her, still dribbling thick white sperm. He seemed to be falling asleep. Crash shoved him, and he rolled off of her, his wet dick slapping against his thigh. She felt the muscles in her vagina contract and expand.

Funny, the nausea was passing. She watched him tuck himself back into his soiled boxer shorts, and pull his pants back up. He smiled, embarrassed, and lumbered off down the dark row past all the other clients and empty benches. It was like a series of polaroids flipping before her eyes all of a sudden, a long film of stills. There was the constant slapping sound of wet thigh against membrane, a refrigerator hum in the middle of the night. Glass door sliding open with a click, the sound of money dropping into slots.

Marina is shaking her, suddenly they're on a swing. Singing the first verse of every song they know. It's almost dark, Marina's hair is chestnut, shooting straight out behind her, orange sparks against the twilight sky. Her voice is high, sweet. Crash realizes that Marina has been binge-ing and purging again. There are the tiny tell-tale red dots under her eyes, blood vessels broken from the strain.

It is Easter Sunday. Tears roll down Crash's face.

Portent

I keep thinking
this Jesus candle

is my drink.

David's Glasses

I'm taking a hot bath scented with eucalyptus oil, reading a nightmarish novel written by another author who died from taking too much heroin. She describes her mother as a graceful stranger, starry. She had a disturbing childhood, full of fear. I was afraid of the dark. I still am. David's glasses rest on the side of the tub. They are old, light gold frames that curve, lenses round. Antique.

John Cale on the radio sings Dylan Thomas. "Do not go gentle into that good night." Perhaps I should write poems that rhyme, like I used to. Sang the sun and cried. Nevermore.

I cannot bear to let my eyes linger on David's glasses, resting gently placed on the side of the tub. I am overwhelmed with emotion at the sight of them. I am gripped with the pain of loving him so much. When he holds me, it is unlike any kindness I have ever felt, as adult or child. I can't believe another human being can love me honestly, unconditionally. I am afraid. David is pure light. His chest is a barrel, a blond wooden barrel of light pouring through it. I am afraid.

Lately I have needed his touch. I have needed his arms around me in love. I am terrified of his flesh, so familiar. His flesh is my flesh. The soft and hard places. His toes curved up against mine. We are entity, two bodies. We belong. I am afraid.

One night before a concert I was tired, and thinking, "I'm not saying anything. I must be boring him to death." At which point he leaned over and said, "You are so much fun to be with. I never have to explain anything to you."

I think of my grandmother. She and my grandfather had a wonderful love. This has been written on everyone's faces, on the innocent children's faces of their daughters, both married to cruel and critical men. "Why?" On the faces of their sons, married to competitive wives. "How can it be so?"

When my grandfather died, one could not have entered the chapel where we all grieved without saying to themselves "This was a wonderful love." I can't imagine ma ma moving around inside their house, hands brushing across the closed piano, the coldness of the kitchen table top. His empty bed.

I have the crossword puzzle books he used in the hospital the day he died. I have tapes of them singing and telling stories in the car. I have pictures of him as a baby, a child, a teenager. A man with a whole life before I was born.

I am in love with a man who had a whole life before I was born. Maybe that was the year they realized his vision was wrong. The year of the new bike, the baseball glove. I am looking at his glasses on the side of the tub. He lies in bed reading *Look Homeward, Angel.* He squints. His mind is so good.

I am over the worry of other women. That's nothing. You think you're home free when you find mutual love. You think that you're home free when you find that all the trust that was ever destroyed in you from having your heart laid open by incompetents has been restored.

I don't want to be left with David's glasses.

Cat Boy

Catboy glides in on little fog
feet
bursts in like sun ball
super nova kitty
bossanova
salsa
kitty
mi picante amor
kitty
boom
chick
a
boom
boom boom
Catboy kill a lizard
Catboy kill a bird
Catboy grin
come lick me in bed
come curl up against my back
Catboy come sit in my lap
come listen while mama sings
and plays guitar
come listen
while daddy plays bass
and harmonica
come listen while daddy sits in the sun
Catboy come
Catboy come
Catboy knows all

Catboy genius cat,
model cat,
sharp orange sun cat
triangle green bubble eye
cat
Catboy stare at a bug on the ceiling cat
every cell in his body leaning
toward the ceiling
riveted
predator
killer cat
'/ typing cat
front door's open cat
skin cat
muscle cat
dirt cat in the street
dirt cat in the sun
devil cat scatters in the middle of the night
devil cat clings to the screen outside the bedroom window
when he wants in
and we let him
in
Catboy boy
cat
catch a bird
sleep in your own bed
come rest
come rest on my breast
cat
while I read
watch me read
cover the next word on the page
with your paws

purr like a drill
warm my skin
hurricane under my ribs
with your glowing
curve spine
feline
sanguine
languid
long
picture a lean cat stretched out
squinting into the sun
Cat
bring me your magic
be in the room with me
little warm blooded breathing spirit
Sphinx
wise blooded
little magic mysterious animal
fill a room with your cat voice
your cat purr
you warm the room
kiss the room when you walk in it
with sound
everybody knows
soothe me
caress me with the back of your head
in my palm
Cat
you know me
and I feed you
you feed me
and we often share popcorn
papaya
beer

Catboy killed a bird,
ripped out its intestines with relish
right in front of me.

Mmm, mmm, lip smacking
cat jaw

Mama's heart chamber bones are too big
to tear out with little cat teeth
so come here,
tiny baby
and give mama a kiss.

Joan Bright:
stroganoff,
Brahms

Joan,

I entered your life in the midst of
the week of the gun,
night of the graveyard
red patent heels and

"I needed to lose"

We are women.

We shit together.

fun Joan

vatican

HENRY MILLER'S
eye, joan

july, joan

august wind
creaks

rip the heart right out of my chest
ocean upon ocean of

we laugh

Joan, Bright and Dark

Joan's gun
is loaded

Joan's phone
is off the hook

you'll miss the party
but you won't be sorry

I can count my good women friends on one hand.

I love a man
dear to you

celebrate with acrobats,
fleurs

Turkish
Spanish

costumer Joan

made jewelry for a bomb shelter
macaroni and glue

the fat actress popped a seam
hung over, forgot to sew it back
white flesh dress pinned

I must have sleep

this is the story of

so many of my friends have died
how to read in bed
among artifacts

Armenian tea set
bronze
bright orange Kali
jack o lantern face
paper sculpture in a cold fireplace

the mastery of Janet's hand in the paint

is
evident.

strokes of fire
light green
a whole wall

Yes you told me
your beautiful crazy cousin died

a beautiful blonde Mexican girl

a sad new year

another armful of drugs

another Morro Bay twilight,

surf against black steeple rock
igneous
cold

*Hey, did you hear how
Joan and Art hotwired the car?*

Everyone was angry.

and Joan
I can't bear to read
Play It As It Lays.

It's a vacant valley ranch-style house
with ghosts.

meet us at El Conquistador!

I don't remember how I got home

smile at the blond Mexican waiter

they all have dimples
they love us
sitting outside among the vines

there's cowboy poetry on the radio. liz

well, you need to write a book

it's about your life:
a woman in drag

I almost can't be around Billy, either
you can tell the cancer's hurting him
he refuses to stop moving

but he said
his life is cinematic,
panoramic
and the whole time,
he hears the perfect soundtrack

yes but he'll leave without the directions
and I hate being lost

I hate living here
lost

you're my family, Joan.

plastic baby red
fake fur fez toilet paper cover
on your head
fake blood
on your chest

is that you, Joan?

it's me
carpet burn on my elbows

I was sucking the cock of a boy named Smear,

I think

ah, bliss!

the saga of
the
raga
the
mandala
candelabra
sandal

my head's
my feet
spinnin'

joan dark:
horse verse
obsess

A horse
we noted
this

thing we

have in common

bitten

leaning against the cabinets

vodka and dark sauce

swaying

In a restaurant, later, you spoke of the dead:
"Imagine them at their party. It must be one big song"

I entered my life wearing innocence, fire

in the midst of my
jean seberg obsession
my
joan of arc fix
cessation

painted tin DEVIL at your COLLARbone

chills

dungeon

red
Joan

Joan defiant,
Joan sad
woman's eyes/hips

forward

LATIN

rolling slowly forth and back
brick wall eyes burning

A horse for Joan.

a poem, no muse
leonora carrington
mina loy
duchamp
the bit
duende
muse
terrible
infant
blood red teeth and lipstick

lips tight ribbon of teeth
bloody marie
the three maries

CATHOLIC

sick

tombstone hairdo
windswept back,
ribs

No more religious ceremonies should be held in
"the cave with the horse pictures"

ancient pagan horse-worship

don't look me in the mouth,
I was born in jail
I am a master of fine arts
literate,
bitter
smoked
m.d.a.

the White Mare

epona

leukippe

divine horse

wept for votre tres belle cousine
white horse
couchemare
come true

Sleipnir, symbol of the gallows tree

it was you there
watching you
with

A Christian prejudice against queens

hobby-horse

*"The 'horse' enables the shaman to fly
     through the air, to reach the heavens"*

funerary horse
pallor

His ghost needed a ride to heaven

High-chested rope
gilded
stone
galloper
highness

Odin's own death-and-resurrection drama,
leading the dead thru the sky on
cloud-colored horses

Hindu dying gods often assumed horse-shape

the October Horse

heralding a season of
drinking
silk to sleep in
mourning

breath

Mare-headed Demeter
dry earth
grassless
singing my body
on hands and knees

My dilemma has become
this river.

three streams
running up the backs of my calves
sacred
calves

eaten

Man-eating mares
in the night,

joan

yes, run for office!

yes, imbibe spirits
vapour
replete with symptom

"no-one's got MY back against a wall"

I'm learning to fall in love with painting

WHY did you quit?

There ARE flowers there

diana
bellona
artemis
athens
etc.

the warrior girl enters the sundial of her life
stilled
without turning
the brightness
is cast

You Can't Keep A Good Woman Down
—A re-interpretation of the magazines.

Urgent as a sky is blue,
you can't keep a good woman down.

These are the politics of my dream:

1. Crush Beauty
2. Spit it out!
3. Plagiarize — go naked for a sign!
4. Appropriate when appropriate
5. Follow and run on angel's clocks
6. Command them to call you, *now*.

A city is beaten back into the Earth.
Places I've longed to visit, burning still.

Baghdad, Yugoslavia,
Los Angeles

these days I've

"a head drilled clear through
  so that dark falls through it"

the darkness of
Elisabeth
in exile

Return to thine own house!

chase me

Your good women will not wait!

A *real* 36D,
my hair is my art

O, to swim again in Texas rivers!

Return!

because if i become incomprehensible i will not be heard

Stumbling.

because I bought the Beauty Myth.

Hey, "the author is gorgeous"

because "Wow, I'm sick of doubt!"

because I hold things dear, like satiny pages

because I read

"A woman is often measured by the things she cannot control"

I read

"Statistics may lie when it comes to women, but they are very
important when it comes to *shoes*"

Figures count.

Beauty doesn't count if you're a theorist.

We keep repeating a line from a book,
a girl "born of a light bulb,"
a sundial.

- she is standing in the middle of her life -

palm of thorns,
the wrong words

What's wrong with you?

"This is eye color that cares!"

I'm an Iron Maiden,
a rock wife
a Stones woman
cinched

without a body

I'm nobody.

A human error.

I read

"While some faces look fine, others look flawless"

Even in death,
she was beautiful.

Looked Good For Her Age.

it's a good thing he can't see her face

I'm stumbling.

No woman has walked this path before me.

Urgent as a sky is blue,
religion is random
sickness covert
precise

If you are beautiful,
you will pay.

I read
"Express your style in three words or less"

Fearless and Ready!

Women: I present you power, here.

because "Wow, I'm sick of doubt!"

all I could think about
was how I'd let down everyone if I lost,
even God

Vessel
"Every woman is a vessel."
—Patti Smith

Used to you could fuck.

Used to you could suck, lick, taste, fist, nibble, chew, bang,
boink, boff, ball and *swallow*

but now.

"The prostitutes were fingered for THIS crime."

Someone's got to be guilty.

Someone's got to carry the sickness inside them

someone's got to be

the womb
tomb
the chalice

girl spreads her legs inside the palace
the temple of Isis
is

consecrated with

my tears.

The tears of whores.

Pretty women.

Don't even say
/blood.

Don't even think
/fluid.

"I didn't start the beauty contest, but I can't ignore it either.."

There's no escape from the parade.

A silent movie majority.
Rated lust in the city of close-ups.

A woman is viewed through a hole.

This is the night of
the zipless fuck
the seamless screw
the dreamless sleep

cold naked shoulders above the sheets
wet below
with sweat

Wash everything clean:

brains

hands

$20,000 cars

your stinky snatch

This becomes the womanly
interior scroll

the message
in *this* bottle
(pointing to crotch)

Listen!

A vessel is a structure designed to travel on water and carry
people or goods, a ship or a boat

a colonizing expedition
of rapists

Christopher Columbus' mother
was

a hollow receptacle
for his father.

Females receiving.

Return to sender!

We know that it is easier to prevent conception before the
sperm leaves a man's body than after it has entered a woman.

I repeat.

We know that it is easier to prevent conception before the
sperm leaves a man's body than after it has entered a woman.

Why all the experiments?

I can kill you with one whisper to the right god of sky

Tonight I'm wearing Crystal Ball cologne.

I see into the future
and I take
what I want.

Litter
(Sorry, Ma, My *Biographical* Clock Is Ticking)

I write then roll the paper up
into little balls,
crunching

constant writing and rolling and crunching

the mountain of paper
the dead sea
I'm swept up in

"When are you going to make me a grandmother?"

I dream of genealogy!

I want to tell the story of *my* grandmother:

bastards, gris-gris and mojo
Our Lady of Prompt Succor
St. John the Baptist
the one real love
cancer, drunk driving, floods, hurricanes

"I wonder who has the violin?"

land deeds in French
Sweet Georgia Brown
a black cauldron with its legs cut off

when will you become
the member of the wedding?

"it's *too* southern!"

Ou est que t'est parti oui mon bon vieux mari?

matron of honor
old maid of honor
a flower *girl*

I wanted to give birth

to literature

Adolescent girl strides forth
"with shadows on her chest"

Welcome to the ranks
welcome you
progenitor of the bloodline

stay safe on the streets

"men can no longer protect you"

well I can!

I built an altar
to Artemis
Marie
Melanie
Aphrodite
Elder

"the *Wide* Goddess."

I just kept eating.

I wanted to be chosen.

St. Anne, St. Anne,
Get me a man!

I read where
a bishop gnawed the arm bone
of Mary Magdelene's corpse for strength

this is weird

I eat dream-journey narratives,
feminist books
the sky

I see through heaven's eye

and my eyes are bigger than my tummy

one more item on my plate

with the eggs...

A baby?

In *this* world?

I am bitter about the litter.

I feel disguised.

"Back then, women sometimes had to chew through the umbilical cord when they delivered."

From Louisiana to Los Angeles.

Just living here is upping Dante's ante.

City of skinny women.
Lifting belly women.
People on the verge of being stylish.
Where your only other option is surgery.

I watch these bastards in their Mercedes throw trash out the window, and I'm thinkin'

>*Stop leaving your crap for someone to pick up after you!*

I AM NOT YOUR MOTHER.

The baby bomb generation.

Pulling the pin on our planet, dammit!

Planet Parenthood. The ex*plosion* is the message.

This is an epitaph for ecology!

A prayer for pollution to cease.

>When *I* was a kid, we sang songs,
>we pitched in to clean up America!

I was a safety patrol then, too.

I kept

thinking everything would be OK.

I burned my face off in the sun,
in less time
than it used to take.

I am NOT your mother.

SOMEBODY *PLEASE* PAY THE JANITORS!

"Ashes rise
above the typewriter
a black silver sky of broken film"

smoke curls
angel wings
licking the pavement

and I realize

we are wasted here.

Empress Nag

Empress Nag!
Was a horse lover at fourteen.
Empress Nag!
Is a full-blown bitch.
A sluh-t.
So what!

Don't tell ME how to parallel park!

A woman to sustain,
my name
I mean
her name
requires no translation,
spoke itself
NAG
is the first word taught to babies even to the present day.

Mama, ma mere, mi madre

She sings the war song of the Amazons:

(Overlapping slightly)

To arms, to arms, the warlike fare,   *Her arms, her*
                                             arms, long and fair
As our heroick charms,   *as hemlock trees*
With martial echo's fill the air   *with marital echoes fill*
                                             the air

<table>
<tr><td>

Inviting unto arms.
If ever their bright eyes beheld

A chorus like to ours;
Or saw themselves so far excelled

By women's more heroick powers.

</td><td>

inviting arms...
If ever their bright
eyes beheld
a chorus like ours
or saw themselves how
hard we kick
their butts with our
womanly heroick
powers they would
FREAK.

</td></tr>
</table>

Take back the street, mom.

"Someone's got to give you your first gun."

Nice girls don't shoot.

Oh yeah?

Throughout history, the naginata was women's weapon of choice for close combat.

naginata: a Japanese weapon used predominantly by women. From the ancient Empress Jingo Kogo onward, Japanese women have been noted for warrior valor.

Some famous naginata
– dentata –
practitioners include

(loosely translated from the Japanese)

Rejoice   *Joyce James*
Haiku   *Colette*
It took Gawking   *Joan of Arc*
Combingly   *Mina Loy*
Taco Cabana Homer   *Billie Holiday*
Massacred Hollow   *Mae West*
Tamarind Hind   *Maya Deren*
Tengo No Tombstone   *Marie La Veau*
Tomorrow Goshen.   *Elizabeth Cotten*

Empress Nag
gave her daughter a revolver
Empress Nag
revolution is now
Empress Nag awaken
the killer
inside her *(me)*
words won't do it
they want poems pouring forth from her mouth,
from all cracks and openings and for cutting
they see her *(me)* as cunctipotent
journeying without escort
they want her for birth
(words come out of the belly)
want her out on the street

listen:

Every woman is a vessel.

listen:

My tears
were the tears of whores

listen:

The death goddess, who also gave birth to everything,
carried plague.

*In Germany, Annie Oakley shot a cigarette out of Kaiser
Wilhelm II's mouth.*

A snake-haired demoness,
I fell in love with an anonymous bass player.

I feasted on the flesh of defeated warriors,
I bathed my blade in blood to the hilt,
I made dinner at six.

I appointed numerous women to highly placed positions.

I'm Tom-rig by day,
Empress Nag by night.

*Tom-rig: an Elizabethan tomboy or roaring girl. The quintessen-
tial tom-rig was Moll Cutpurse. See also Long Meg.*

Man eating mare in the night,
nag
snaggle-tooth crone
cauldron
thief, Moll Cutpurse, a pick-pocket
stockbroker

Head of the CIA

You'll do as I say

I'll shoot out the lights
rob you in the dark in overalls
I am and I can be gone

biting into a beating heart,
the warrior swallows bravery

I am
a pelvic bone stretched over North America,
a drum
Mare-headed Demeter
dry earth
grassless
singing my body
on hands and knees
I am and I can be gone
like lightning was
like lightning was
and I will come
come
and go
go
again.

YES, RUN FOR OFFICE!

the warrior girl enters the sundial of her life

stilled
without turning
the brightness
is cast

The Devil's Playground

I entered my life wearing innocence.
I've lost that here.
It's a Blake thing.

"She is standing in the middle of her life"
in Devil Town. The Devil's Playground.

Speaking Devilese.

Run, devil, run!

Los Angeles,
heaven.
Los Angeles,
hell.

I love it, I hate it, I love it, I hate it.
It loves me, it loves me *not*.

Los Angeles,
it rains or it pours.
Los Angeles,
what I have is mine,
and what I *want* is yours.

A symphony for the devil.
I got a date with mi "Duende".

Los Angeles,
upping Dante's ante.
Los Angeles,
a birth through fire.
Los Angeles,
a trial by living.

Los Angeles,
living is wet.

Be a piss factory, share a bathroom.

The waste of water is/
the cough in my lungs
now we are having the conservation conversation!

Remember, there are ways to live safely,
but *look* like you're doing it dangerously.

"Gettin' down with the dirty scene."

Los Angeles!

Hell A.

Devil Incorporated. Live music and dead muses. The "ask
and ye shall receive town." Be careful what you wish for. I
wanted to be alone. Banished from San Francisco and in exile.
I wanted to write for TV. There is a certain revenge in politi-
cal incorrectness. There's gold in them there hills.

Los Angeles, the crucible.

Mothers descending into Hell to save their daughters,
failing.

That which does not kill me makes me a stranger.

I can't breathe.

Diving deeply into the wreck, swimming in a pool of
schmooze sharks. Brush your teeth, then *lie* through them.
Betrayal becomes routine. We become what we resist and it is
for this reason that I believe in good and evil.

So what.

*It is the feet of the devil that halt a man in his tracks. Idleness the
guide animal, the nurse of sin. A hag with an ax to grind. Makes
young people sleep. The slaves of sloth are punished by having
their legs and feet broken. This is the deadly sin. Cessation.*

Los Angeles, a list.

I'm the Cajun middle class hetero safe sex master of fine arts
ex-Catholic pseudo Buddhist abused child — punk rock was
my life! — pissed off feminist *believin'* in the sisterhood
detoxin' echinacea and goldenseal voodoo witch carnivore of
vague ethnic origin: COME SEE ME READ.

Mother I hear your accent,
your soft Texas voice.
You are the stars and the grace that I miss.

Texas ground I'd like to kiss,
the small sky over Los Angeles
burns.

Truth is that river you cannot enter
twice, the Gulf of Mexico opens before us.

The borders are closed.
Down like dominoes.

Our dilemma has become
this river.

L.A. River, man-made
like everything else.

I must somehow become the sundial,
I must seek
to be still,
clear.
Joan of Arc clear
ah, Joan

give me the present

it's Rosemary's baby shower,
let's go!

I wanted to give birth
to literature

"Your poems, though erudite and witty, are a bit long."

Well goddamn, doesn't anyone *read?*

What *did* happen to Kerouac?

His portrait taped to her steering wheel, a woman writer
moves forward through the desert. Cherry pits in the ashtray.

"You think you're such an artist!"

Run, devil, run!

"You don't have to go to school to be a poet, you know."

*"the imitator is a professional mourner, with no motive but
money. the words burn, but there's no warmth, and no broken-
open-ness"*

"You're a better writer than I am...I'm jealous!"

Run devil, run!

I shiver into particles.

The words are written inside me.
The poems become the journey.

Los Angeles, I love you.
Los Angeles, I hate you.
City of my Saturn return.

Los Angeles, I love you.
Los Angeles, I hate you.
City of hotdogs.

City of the sun.

I've passed lost girls I cannot reclaim,
faceless thieves,
blind men telling mountain ranges

I burn names in effigy,
become the phoenix I'd predicted.
New Year's Eve in Arizona.

I entered my life wearing innocence.
I've lost that here.

Devil Town. The Devil's Playground.

I read what's been written inside me.
A love song, an ode, a eulogy.

Tighten the reins.

Conjure great weather.

Mother, here I come!

Hopeless, fearless, faithful.

Ready.

I Didn't Write A Riot Poem

I didn't write a riot poem. I'm not from here, what do I care if the whole thing gets gutted by fire? Sure, I've got a couple of friends who live in South Central, but I hardly ever go *there*. Kamikaze city, just stick the knife into your belly till the flames spill out. I didn't move here to raise a family, I moved here to get a piece of what I want and then I'm splitting, WITH the money. It's not like LA is proud of itself or its history — past, present, or future — they even tore down the Brown Derby, the world's most famous celebrity restaurant! Gotta make way for those new parking lots. Think of the people who have died here. Peg Entwistle. She's the girl who jumped from the Holly-wood sign. Suicide is a way of life in Los Angeles. I've even con-sidered it myself, but I would hate for this hell hole to be the last thing I see.

You gotta die to be born here. Then you rise like a Phoenix over skid row, over a downtown skyline and you sail, you sail, you scream "Ha, ha, you living motherfuckers! I win! I win!" and then you roll with the flames until you are fire. They'll raise a statue in your honor. They'll celebrate your unpublished sym-phonies at the Bowl. Your tomb will gather followers for 50 years, people who weren't even born yet when you croaked. You will whisper from your deathbed, *"Now it is time to cross the shifting sands."* You will have created Oz, a whole pantheon to prop you up after you're gone.

All the Best Ones Are Taken
"Some deaths take forever."
—Marilyn French, *The Women's Room*

A conversation with the living.
Teach me how to speak.

"How's your health?"

How's your ancestor's song, Liz?
Is it coming along, Liz?
Are you crying like water?
Are you thinking in tones?

remember your dead loves,
buried in sand —
are you aware?
the wind shifts
the shapes disappear,
it's like they never lived

"And the phone bill, Bill?
Rehearsal space rent?
I called because I heard a tooth in the back of your jaw is
aching,
hello?

o, the blue day!
now our own children are strangled
down in the bubbling quadrangle

"How's your blood count,
  Vlad?"

How's New Jersey?
I've heard your parents are born again.
Do you eat
processed meat?

I walked all the way east from
the west, speaking poems
I felt the words spill
from my teeth
like water

I was terrified of the man I loved.
We kissed without tongues
we rubbed our faces raw
every morning.

And man cannot live
on salad alone.

Hello, Joan.
A woman is off the hook.
You'll miss the party
but you won't be sorry.

*—la reina cries like water
on the phone—*

What's your number?
  What's the number
of your cell?
How many T-cells are there in your jail?"

I can either count my losses or my blessings.

Look around.

a yellow moon full of empty chairs
shelves with books spilling over
in the comfort of your own home
or a coffee house

one's in the basement
mixing up the medicine

one's lying on the pavement
drinking up the sun – he's one

you see

all the best ones
New York City, a student of
art history
sucked a lot of dick for fun

all the best ones

dying in Austin
but you never knew it
remember his skin,
broken black horn rims,
masking tape glass
a beat poet and I never knew it

look around you now
before you know it

all the best ones
Michelangelo, Bob

just cuz
we liked speed
we need
to lose?

all the best ones
V. not you

this is a painting by someone
you'll never know
and even Harry died of natural causes
untangling wet junkie poet hair
from the side of the bed
all the best ones
the djs
the dancers
photographers
all
Cookie
your landlord
the buddhists
musicians
spanish
Michael
the actors
Al
I don't want to live
in a nation that's invisible,
either

as the lipless media claims it's done
and godless preachers load their guns
all the best ones
the best ones
your father,
your mom
all the best ones
the best ones
the best ones are
gone

Cindy Crawford Dream

I dreamed i was in a grocery store and Cindy Crawford came in and robbed it. She shot Alison Turner, my childhood best friend, who was trying to run out the front door. I went over and grabbed Cindy and said, let's get out of here! So we ran to her van...or was it mine? And we kept leaving all kinds of evidence...evergreen needles...She was beautiful and she was actually naked! It was kind of sexual. She was like a doll. I kept telling her she had to turn herself in and she was too scared to do it. I kept telling her that the longer she went and the more evidence we left the more trouble we'd both be in. And that the whole world would just love the opportunity to tear her apart.

Feminine Manifesto
—for Michelle T. Clinton and Linda J. Albertano

This is a feminine manifesto.
Nice.
Pretty.

This is
an ode to the power of pussy,
a prayer for a dickless sort of world:
both women and men.

An elegy for "cunt" being a dirty word.

A demand for a womb of one's own!

The right to bare.

Here is my 20 point plan, what I suggest we do socially,
politically, poetically, economically, yea metaphorically, in
order to form a more perfect union:

1. Crush Beauty.
2. Spit it out!
3. Quit looking at me!
4. Remember your mother every time a sun sets. Send *her* the
   card on your birthday.
5. Fear of filing is common! Unless you're a writer, don't
   learn to type!
6. The next Star Trek captain gets to be a woman.
7. Keep Secret Notebooks.

8. Take over airwaves!

9. Teach little girls Aikido...*along with* how to make food.

10. Only do work which is life-affirming, thereby permanently changing human consciousness. Remember : DADA affects DNA.

11. Turn to the *poets* for accurate information. Not the scientists, not the press.

12. Remember: sexual repression leads to bad politics.

13. Demand free tampons from the state!

14. Worship the Wide Goddess. Black Athena. Your only other option is surgery.

15. You may say: I WILL be angry until RAPE is no longer tolerated here!

16. The term "male bashing", when applied to poetry, is invalid. Consider the statistics. Linda Albertano said this. She was right.

17. Remember our foremothers. Name three of yours now.

18. Write down your dreams.

19. Write 70 country and western songs. Transpose every song you know to G, C, and D. Even Blondie.

20. And please. Write your own manifesto!

My Country, *My Cunt*

Stinks, *smells like night blooming jasmine.*
In trouble, *gets me in trouble.*
On fire *on fire.*
Feels like a riot,, *feels like a rainstorm.*
Fills the earths full of holes, *feels like a hole in the earth.*
Humiliating, *makes me proud to be woman.*
The fear of women giving birth, *making birth possible.*
Worships cock, *wants cock — sometimes.*
Bloodthirsty, *blood.*

Doesn't care if women come, *wants all women to come and
come as much as they possibly can — without jeopardizing the
fact that they may have to get out of bed once in a while.*

Warlike by nature, *warlike when necessary.*
Famine, *feast.*
Wants to put its fingers into everything,
wants fingers. Wants freedom.

Was a foreign home to Salvador Dali,
is homefront for Inanna and Kali.

Believes that it's the center of the universe,
IS the center of the universe.

My country, *my cunt.*

Sent Me To The Hospital

"the whole...room...was swirling...her lips...were still...
curling..."
— Marianne Faithfull

You sent me to the hospital
blue bottle went spinning off the top of my head
took my fist and swung it back far as I could
took my fist and put every last ounce of Amazon goddess
steamroller big warm hot thunder thigh mama hot fat breast
fertility hunter goddess bow and arrow meat mama wide
woman weight into it took my fist to your face right between
your eyes, which by the way, are just a little too close
together, Georgia boy.

both went black
broke your nose

and if it had been the olden days you know the olden days of
darkness when all women were still just virgin, mother, whore
they woulda ripped my uterus right out
cuz I was hysterical, honey
it woulda been history
they'da hysterecto-me!

All my feminist marxist pacifist books floated
up to the ceiling
and didn't come down till January 18th
the day after the quake
 – all her earthquake life –
all my feminist books came crashing down around me

and now I can read them again
cuz I didn't have time to think then

I didn't have time to think about all the lyin' cheatin' scum
bad surgery job on the heart, doc!
I sent flowers to your funeral
but you sent me to the hospital
and the real doctor who examined me was young and cute
and I think he kinda liked me

I never thought I would be a statistic
a wailing violin a number on a page a
inner city woman a war torn woman
domestic violation in my own home

sent me to the hospital called the cops
called my mom
coulda gone to jail
coulda told the cops it was your new cocaine fixation
your new you

both eyes black
to match your leather
jack

ooh baby baby
if I could
I'd take you back!
If you'd return my calls
if you had the balls
I'd have you back and
I'd fuck you so raw you'd bleed.

But there's sore bones in my skull,
in my fist
and I'm thinkin'
every time that
skinny bleach blond boob job coke whore bimbo groupie sees
your face when you got ready to stick your dick into her
murky, parched pussy she sees the Mark of Liz Belile!

Yeah!

You sent me to the hospital and I am
well, well, well.

Now go to hell.

The New Feminism Is

lipstick lesbian bull dyke global cyberotic parisian asskiss cunt on a pedestal waving a new flag sisterhood of strippers, masters of fine arts harvard law senator kindergarten teacher jemela playwright empress negress cracker bitch chicana in stripes hands on hips raw angles burying a baby in her backyard bleeding for years uterus clenched in shock bad news seeping weeping on shoulders soft sharp head newspaper headlines screaming serial killer! serial killer! i want the women, the killer said, smiling, opening fire she opens her knees to give birth and to receive on her hands and knees crawls across border patrol "please don't let them kill us" civil war woman is the faggot of the world the fear of math disgrace of language arts fine tongues full on a muscle flinch twitch so many women so few orgasms so many men so little satisfaction man hating mare in the night, nag horse headed cult of the sensual mother drums outright talking liquid poesie oh my sonnet is on tight tonight dull eyes pay to play every woman is a vessel is a musician breast cancer can't have her we march we march we set the world on fire with speech sojourner truth's broad back picked to the bone every time i lay on my back i am magdelene, josephine, simone, angela, alice, ntozake, athena if only i could be her hard body her arched rib her linen fish net corset statue of liberty i lost my son to a gun there is no joy like georgia o'keefe a desert crone sail phoenix after centuries tied to a brittle map laid folded inside a chest between swinging breasts a perfect bound book written in the body a writer tells it we are here

H.D.
—for L.C.

Coming out of this misery
among red rocks
and strange sunrendered scenery
I find the place
where poetry begins
and begins again to mean much to me:
H.D.

Her pomegranate mouth
her ruby body
her sharp smart hair
the top of her head
steel grey lines
a graduate's cap
an alchemist's robe
woolen, black
bright eyes, soft obsidian
voluptuous magic words
lifted
turn toiling, boiling in turns
in her mouth
spit out the seeds
plant trees

to the future

Polishing the Bayonet
random line trance files and the alphabet method

I met a rapist in the war.

old soldiers weep
by nights
by nights explosion is
cancer,
smoking

snake-haired demoness
so many of my friends have died

assassinated

Thin rope Years War. This is a dream.

Soon more than you need

SHE met a rapist in the war

Shelling
Come out of your shell, little girl
white flesh dress pinned

they see her as cunctipotent
naked vein facing the world

a show ghost

just write just write
god
never married
ruthlessness
sacrifice
sad day
sad empty

too sudden to do

shoulder head stretch

Tamarind
why idle if overflow

was liking waiting around
the writing come

Saturday night carjack at the corner of Hyperion and
Rowena, where I turn everyday to go home my little peach
house with its white picket fence

crazy creamy cream

so what

shiny
ship or boat

don't shake your hair like that

don't cry
my darkling
my darling dear

Brush your teeth
then lie through them

Betrayal becomes routine

STUMBLING
stumbling

a hand sideways to the back of the head
a hatchet hand to the back of the head
a horse

fun release jail

with me in it,
with shadows on her chest
with stung eggs

o pity the old, he's departed;

horse head jaw
in their
a desire for souvenirs,
a dog collar,
a dried sea walking
a drum
a dry
era of
seaweed

Catboy leap over the fence
Catboy kill a bird

thrust forward under a jaw

piss warm mad deposits there
 catgut peter piper,
 pitches in

she was the star

Sweet Georgia Brown
sweet
sweet
sweet girl
obey

she was crazy

I dream of genealogy.

I eat dream-journey narratives,

the tied men mouthing

Tired of being in love with the hero
I find the place
macaroons and glue

Silver Lake.
THE DEVIL'S PLAYGROUND:

side fun realize

A mannish woman who strides, hips first, up and down
Hyperion.
smoke curls

I burned my face off in the sun
this is the way the writing begins

her sharp smart hair
killing
I wonder who has the violin?

Hell A
Automatic wiring

spilled her blood in the Sahara

lobelia anyway there

so there us
stormy messages are across to say oh just measure

tease here
solar

I was a safety patrol then, too.

The cold alone is penetrating

it was an idea which was inextricably bound up with

horribly

provided a model for earthly government

spread mist in the belly open

steel rod neck
I am NOT

I just kept eating
floods and hurricanes

her arms

her arms

small loam
mad
see west;

creamy element net
full of foam and mist

Get me a man!

fun Joan

the mountain

the notion of life as continuity and succession

love really dark
when will outright become what they thought you all
were
would be

MY BIOGRAPHICAL CLOCK IS TICKING.

lets be smart and start

lies

life

I am bitter about the litter.

I hang upside down in a tree
I have headaches now
from fingertips to knees

I broke bright cycle

Come out of your shell

little girl.

There's going to be war.

some cry
groaning as the world is pulled apart

guise
go

go
 don't pay no attention that man alive in the like of sea

go among artifacts

spit out the seeds

die
die
die

die

dies

hair
department

dear old man so we
cast her spell across the table,

decade wrenching hear long

Every woman is a vessel

Come out of your shell, little girl

Someone's got to be the womb

crunching

erotic zone

like a cellstring jackal
jalapeno okay so surreal
is twenties
decade
wrenching
hear long ago
dirge
worth

don't write
whore

whose name means by-night
whose name means "Starlight"

SIN was here

Creole
hey I don't know maybe

direct contact with God

so there that year
was liking waiting around
was truly Cleopatra

she bathed her blade in blood to the hilt

EXT. LOS ANGELES — NIGHT

facing the fear

FADE UP:

in a grin
create

I met a rapist in the war

The "ask and ye shall receive town"

her name

I can still feel
our dead are
idle
our planet,
out on the street

strange sunrendered scenery

teeth

after

AFTERLIFE

deepens you appear
hag

Haiku

encourage this

a vessel is a structure designed to travel on water and carry
people or goods
for the fingers
friend
breton desnos
breton desnos rimbaud no breton
breton desnos rimbaud no breton surreal
bright army now.

Crete mute play

I promise to be
good

a feeling of "something's missing"

his life is cinematic

woolen, black
words won't do it
work
worth

hundreds of thousands of people died

feminist books

she's sleep writing

there's cowboy poetry on the radio Liz

don't have a life

to enjoy all the prerogatives of the god
Jupiter

Christopher Columbus' mother was

I don't know for a second

bastards, gris-gris and mojo

house of bongos
house of conga
house of ants in the sink

I threw away everything

my dolls

Los Feliz

Lost on Angus street, my dream house with cement tiers for steps.

Stop leaving your crap for someone to pick up after you!

Hey
did you hear how

Her pomegranate mouth

be a cup
be at home please
be born there
be gone

Just living here is upping Dante's ante.

three men bend over the engine of an Oldsmobile in the street.

Los Feliz
so close
so hard

retell
come
just realize

let's do this more often
you like it you
so do she

yes your dream sees well

sure death day

are in me vodka jaw ash hair afar

tease here

Saint

City of skinny women.

killed
too powerful to hold or recapture

SHE love it
SHE hate it
SHE love it
SHE hate it

Los Angeles

Los Angeles

the message
warm mad
spots

philosophical research society

Someone's got to be guilty

riot here large
rip the heart right out of my chest

I'm like I'll tell you suffer

It's heavy here.

it's about your life:

pounded in
power regime Crete
anyone makes anymore
apart from the fact that
Aphrodite
appears
don't cry my darkling my darling dear

writer
thief

I want to give birth

Big beefy men in tight little shorts on Griffith Park Blvd.

let me hold you
let me hang you
let me have you here

Past the convent, over the bridge.

it wasn't too easy

inviting arms

love
dark

love lifted out
low demand see,
lust

just write
just we write
let me lightly
okay yes well

matron of honor

doves kissed you

stormy messages are

narrows her

don't write
retell

I'm the Cajun

she dived in the sinewy sea there SHE was here

crazy

songs,

There's going to be war

just for fingers
ode

Lately we fall in and drown

what a year
what a year someone go to
what caused this?

by adult emergence

were the tears of whores

were wrenching
wet dirt mouth

so dreamy wheel
hey dish don't
knowledge maybe
read your lake
let yourself suffer

It ended
as all things must

Too good to be true
this happened fast

He sandblasted her name off his tower

Astro Family Restaurant and TV LOG w/ star photos and
run on sentences by the Greek gossip columnist. "SWM seeks
pretty lady, any race. Also, I have 2 leather jackets for sale."

alchemy yourself down

not really a great writer
eyes
you are yes
SHE was
she was

rama strata
dried sea walking-

sharp broken bones
SHE almost can't be around Billy

either

which gives shape to life
whinny
whispers

MUSIC CUE:
mute

Bite into a beating heart

the saga of

the same drug
the scythe
the serpent biting its own tail

the she demon's mouthing it
the sky back of him deep;

the story of
the symbolism of devouring

 you won't be sorry
you'll miss the party

the dark
the dead are idle
the dead sea
the fat actress popped a seam

SYNOPSIS
Taco Cabana

an alchemist's robe
an enamored alien over crown murder
and a desperate quest

She feasted on the flesh and blood of defeated warriors

 SHE was a fish

he said

woman
woman of lasting

spinnin'

Kafka

The setting is the city
apocalyptic and violent

yes that's right

guise
the sky back of him deep;
there

don't be afraid
alchemy yourself down

ash
ash
ashes rise

SHE wanted to be alone

SHE mean
in her mouth

wrenching
wretch

SHE can't bear to read

the whole time

celebrate with acrobats

write become what they thought you

writer

little girl
that year
gangs on the streets or survivalists gone underground

it's me

it is for this reason that

girl spreads her legs inside the palace

blackness dominating from her

a whole wall
a woman in drag
a woman to sustain

smoke cough on the truth
carpet burn on my elbows
jaws

and later for the displacement of
sacrifice as the sole source of re-creation

and transformation

happy go lucky

in the sisterhood
they all have dimples

poems appear dear

Homer

in Devil Town

there bombed the painter proper

he's where jackals write
his lower jaw entertains us
sufis yes

the member of the wedding
at the head of her army

That which does not kill me

means motif does it mean something

she moved that once

Everyone was angry

everything

evident

ex-Catholic

stormy messages are across to say

warrior swallows bravery

the bloodline
the brevity and intensity of life
the Carnival itself is

I am the tree

slants

why dead are

don't be afraid
don't be serious

"Don't talk back to your mother, girl!"

they were not prepared for the sheer rage that hit them

daughter

create
doubt easy

Please don't tell them where she's gone

don't wait with the light on

panoramic

progenitor of

ecology
"SHE needed to lose"

even on the plane of the divine

She showed you

songwriting

There's gold in them there hills

"She is standing in the middle of her life"

the she demon's mouthing it

voluptuous magic words

the untold lies

night of the graveyard

where jackals were

The Grassy Knoll basement.

I try to speak when angry

to play the part of Saturn

Joyce James

Why Does SHE Keep Falling For Male Men?

I want to say hawthorn

her ruby body

sings bout music

sings the war of song
song of the Amazons:

fun release jail

on extended hands
on my plate
on your chest
on your head

help me

where poetry begins

sickness

for his father

Parenthood

writing lightly

be OK

child

tremble is an epitaph for
tripping

throughout history

its
your first gun

Be careful what you wish for

this bloody ceremony by its simulacra
this is a dream

Smell the air.

dear god

City of my Saturn return

overflows

the hourglass
the idea that each

sort of mom

club

SHE met a rapist in the war

boy let me hold you
boy relax my dear
Brahms

I AM NOT YOUR MOTHER.

hey dish don't

a baby held in the crevice
a baby?
a babyhood face down in the dirt
a bishop
a black silver sky of broken film"
a Blade Runner-like vision

tits

 gone
gone
good

our dead are really idle

breathe into the belly

baby
baby blackout in the forehead
baby sweet
baby sweet pie cake honey boy

Baby's crying in Spanish at the pool

flowers bloom in the heat
jasmine
belladonna
azalea

The thing is
life on earth

throwing trash

overtake time

as it is sleeping

don't be afraid

when the moon hits the sky tonight

jack o lantern face

I'd like to cut

does what

twisting tubular neck

bright eyes, soft obsidian

pretty boy
pretty boy
primordial chaos

weep
weep

another armful of drugs

So what

middle class

Sufis

Saturnalia

audible eek Crete we

Planet

Ou est que t'est parti oui mon bon vieux mari?"

open the flow to the head
open to laugh

consecrated with

Shelling

as well as the colour black
ash
bliss!
ask about what ask
don't ask

To Graph The Sea
—for Eleni

The ocean is a cut-up alphabetical poem.

The question remains

how
to graph the sea?

ocean pummels shore,
indifferent
spray fist

your elegant hands

you were watching you with
hand cupfuls

woman of the well

whose face behind the mask?

                              who holds it loosely

who broke this heart?

what secret is there...

          what did i learn from the sea?

what did i learn from seeing?

wells, springs, lakes, sea-shrines
we think in tones

we cry like water,

waves

water gave birth to spirit

water is life

water

wash me,

underwater

                                              toes in the mud

to drink

tiamat

                         three echoes

themis

the voyeur inside me
the lady of the lake
the baptismal font

                                    the waste of water is
                                     the temple of isis is
                                    the mother-letter m

teach me how to speak
from lack of differentiation

some poetry's green

so what.

sister of the spring

self and mother

                                                        seafoam, carpet

salt to taste

red, black, yellow, white.

read me like a book

pink

pagan water
oh, the sound of water

oh, the blue day!

my tears
                    mermaids murmuring

mary's womb glows

make me new

ma-nu

                                        love stays with a man

living is wet

let it flow from you

kali

is my drink
is

                                                in water?

in less time

i need a drink

i keep thinking

i have a "nature of water"

            i burned my face off in the sun,

i believe in good and evil.

                                        four seas
                                        flow into you

first of the elements

faking the big sea
faking the big c

faced with the mask

drink me
coral shell

blue lines in a face

between self and other

are you sure you want to quit?

        arche, the mother of all things

an image really drawn

an ideogram for waves of water

an open letter

                an event to renumber
                an event to remember

baptism, drowning in life

a flower of blue lines

a dark room's delights

the dark room of the sea
you wrote a book about it, you
Greek allusion
you teller of tales
sonnet

singer
sea kissed
beauty

ahhhhhh.........................

Tourniquet Sun
—a collaboration w/ André Breton

The voyagers traverse the halls,
tombs,
delicate jets

March ate the sun,
the point despairs
the dispossessed roulette ceiling
sees grand arms
sighs beautifully
dancing lakes of man
mainly await money
rivers reverse
falcons of selves
queasy breathing, a migraine of God
the torpedoes are deployed, commence the battle

Oh China, quiet fumes
or Venetians entering in to pour,
 eat,
lay against the joined females naked
proving to eat
see sweetly quite
male, eat bias
the lady ambassador of sculpture
oh, the blank curtain, suns, fond nights of news,
apples on pencils
a ball of innocents, battered sons plead
the lamps are permanent, present

a fiery lieutenant dances less than marionettes
the damned sing under siege, ill with the sun,
leap upon change

Rules:
get liquor,
timbre
nets aren't plural
the promises desire nights
eaten into infinity

Where Is The Light?

I don't understand how my mother can be so unsentimental about my grandmother's house, "The Big House."

"Mother is so attached to that house, I don't get it. I guess it's probably because that was the first nice home she owned. Running water, it had electricity...those old Mines homes are built real well, though, I can tell you that. And do you know there's never been a rotten board on that house?"

The house was made of freshly cut pine, originally built to withstand flooding and extremely humid weather. All of the Mines houses stood at least eight feet off the ground, up on stilts, with concrete steps and alcoves beneath them. I remember going to the Mines site recently with my mother's middle brother, Ken.

It's hard to believe the overgrown brush was a street once. In a photograph, phosphorescent tracers are left behind where homes once stood. During the Depression and after, this place was a paradise for workers. It was a self-contained community, with Whites and Mexican families imported to work the sulfur mines. The Company built sturdy, modern homes for everyone, and a school. In rural Louisiana, where almost everyone was dirt poor, this meant a life of luxury. And sulfur was a thriving business until it was replaced with oil. Then the community dried up. It was a time.

Ken showed me the old bath houses, brick with dirt floors, which had later been converted into a jail. The old bank vault was crumbling. The blacktop where they played basketball. And Crystal Creek, where they swam oblivious to the alligators that must have glided past their bony little bodies. "Every year," Ken tells me, "someone drowned in that creek."

I can practically hear the ghosts. There is quicksand and sulfur bubbling on pond surfaces everywhere. A flock of pelicans, of white cranes rest in low hanging trees on the water's edge. Bird calls ring out over the water. The sun sets, crimson on a black bayou. You can feel the place come alive.

Ken shows me the grass-covered trench in the earth. "This is where 32 Mexican workers died." Some chemical, a deadly gas, had been released and they all died instantly. The company rushed in to cover it up, and the workers' bodies were left in the tunnel under our feet.

The first thing you notice about the kitchen is the huge overhanging fluorescent lamp, like a bar light over a pool table, over the island kitchen table built into the middle of the room. When I was a baby it delighted my Pa Pa endlessly to say, "Bebe, where's the light?" and watch me look up at the light and point. This before I could even walk.

I'm told that I spoke at a very early age. Mom says she'd be toting around this tiny bald thing - they used to tape little pink bows to my head - and we'd be in the grocery store or church or someplace and I'd start to talk to people, ask questions, and they'd stare back at me like I was a freak. "I mean you'd *talk*, to people! It wasn't just baby gibberish, it was complete sentences and paragraphs! They were stunned!"

There's a hole in the ceiling near where the light fits in, a hole that one of my uncles shot with a .22 rifle. My grandpa kept his rifles in the little-used closet right there in the kitchen. We were warned early on not to fool with those guns, which might be loaded. The closet is also where they kept part of Dickie's old train set. Lord knows where they kept the rest of it. It seemed to have disappeared from the face of the earth, like my mother's elusive doll collection. "I don't know, Bebe, maybe it's in a box in the dining room closet." I can smell that train set today, faintly of tin and gasoline. Oil.

Other favorite things were my grandmother's jewelry box, a steel gray office supply box with little plastic shelves. My favorite piece was the fake ruby set with rhinestones. Earrings, necklace, and bracelet.

Ma Ma and Pa Pa's closet was a world of mystery. Pillbox hats, 1950s pointy toed pumps, Pa Pa's tie rack. I always thought that closet was haunted. The lightswitch hid just behind the back of the mirror, so you had to stick your hand behind it to turn it on. And the switch was sideways, rather than straight up and down, so you'd have to reach for it to turn it off.

It was always such a pleasure to go in and kiss Ma Ma and Pa Pa goodnight. Sometimes Pa Pa would let me rub his feet with baby powder. I'll never forget Pa Pa's feet, smooth as silk, curved and knobby, thick yellow toenails and arched toes. I can't stand for my skin to be dry, so it fascinated me that he loved us to put powder on his. He had black, oiled back hair, and dark brown skin with a jaw that jutted forward. A huge crest of a nose, and twinkling black eyes. A perpetual grin. He always looked like an old Indian chief to me. He had a tiny, deep blackhead in one cheek that he'd let us try to squeeze, but it never came out.

At dinner, my ancestors and distant cousins crowded around the table with us. They were as alive to me then as they had ever been, in their own lives. Phillip, who died young choking on a plug of tobacco. He was chawing with his friends behind the barn, and Great Aunt Belle saw him so she decided to sneak up and surprise him. When she clapped him on the back he gasped, and inhaled the plug. He became deathly ill, and my Great Grandma Richard insisted that her husband, "the old drunk", took little Phillip to town in the wagon, left him bundled up there and stopped off at the saloon, drinking all the money he was supposed to spend on the doctor.

Aline, Walter's wife, who was killed by drunk drivers on a good Friday, buried on Easter Sunday. Her daughters, Cheryl and Geraldine, wore the Easter dresses she had made for them to her funeral.

Nunez and Emma, the couple who rode day and night to Opelousas in a carriage to testify and save the life of a Negro man who had been framed for a crime he did not commit. Phys, the sister who had bitten a scar into my grandmother's breast out of jealousy. The baby girl who died of dehydration and broke my Pa Pa's heart for the rest of his life. Hitler, the dog.

When my mother was born my Grandma Lyons held her up to the dog and said, "Hitler, this is Tookie." And he protected her until the day he died, when Pa Pa accidentally rolled an oil drum over him. "Why did they name Mama Tookie?" I wanted to know. Otherwise she was known as Dorothy Ann, but only on paper. My grandmother's eyes get faraway. "You know, we never asked. That was always her name."

And Eugenie, my Pa Pa's mom. She was darker than he was, with black hair and eyes, and our trademark square jaw. I remember her from the nursing home. We loved her so much. Eugenie was passionate, crazy about her husband Grandpa Bos. "I wonder who has his violin?" my grandmother asked my mom, as if they'd ever told me he played. "Oh yes, he was the life of the party with that violin." He was a big man, over six feet tall and two hundred sixty pounds. He lost the family fortune after the Depression, co-signing loans that were never paid back. They owned a few dozen rent houses in Gueydan and Crowley. Eugenie used to dress the dead in Gueydan, the beautiful French town where they lived.

And Drozin, cousin Bertha's husband, who was shot and killed by a stray bullet working in the rice fields. Nearly 70 years later, Bertha's eyes still filled with tears.

This is the beginning of the way to write about your family, to understand your own history and the way you hold your head. Me, I'll keep pointing and being happy every time someone asks me *"Ou est la lumiere?"*

Body Builder Fantasy #301

i wake up eating and i can have all the carbohydrates i want, i get to grow to be the size of godzilla and my arm muscles ripple like ribbons on still water in cold, mountainous lands, and my breasts have shrunk down to the leanest mounds of meat and stay perky and stick straight up even without a bra and my thighs are jaguars crouching at the waterfall my skin is fine and oiled and i'm bursting out of it the indentation where my buttocks meet my hip is deep and i could lay on my side fill it with water and a goldfish or a beta a siamese fighting fish who lunges at a mirror of itself its so full of hate like my empty tummy flat with ridges underneath stretched taut over ridges rows of corn field of wheat opening to sky my neck neck of the amazons hold a whole row of corn put a yoke on it pull a carriage with that neck carry the weight of the world on that neck and when i fuck i am like a fucking machine every inch of my body conditioned for giving birth even the muscles in my vaginal wall are bulging and flexing with every twist and turn and then my old boyfriend's new girlfriend that is the archetype of every old boyfriend's new girlfriend, the universal icon of her comes in to interrupt my dream or my meal or she just walks by and i smash her with one fist i chew her up in my muscular jaw i crush her under a barbell i lift my leg and i kick her ass i send her sailing over a goal post her tit implants pop out and go flying with the impact i smash her with one ankle all you can see are her stick arms and legs kicking back and forth for a minute, then nothing ah yes and then i pluck him out from behind a dark building where he stands quivering, quivering in fear because i am now tyrannosaurus bitch i'm green and i'm mad and i'm so full of rage i eat him up whole i eat 'em up whole all of

'em every last one goes yelling down my throat i throw back my
head my mane flies black curls oil the wind in flames i laugh i
laugh and then when i swallow every muscle in my throat and
jaw ripples and i become warrior blood thirsty sated full open
fridge empty street clean lick the pavement dry i roar i turn into
jewels i turn into living stones i am a vase a jar a pitcher of salt
of cool water spilling over the sides of your mouth a sweet roll
mercury flame a root i wake up eating and i stay hungry

Better Be An Ode To Me

you've got to get up in the morning check yourself you haven't
wet yourself you gotta wake up dry you gotta open your one
good eye and pull out the bad put it back in its box by your bed
you've bled long enough your blind eye that blind eye to love
you gotta turn it gotta put a match under your ass and burn it
you've got to get up in the morning slough off that outer layer
of skin loofah the roofah your mouth you gotta wake up fake
fingernail make up a reason to live you gotta give a good reason
you gotta say god today I am living for food i am living for
good clean fun i'm living for my job for carpal tunnel syndrome
so someone else can sit on his throne though i am the queen
when i'm home when i'm home when i'm alone taking off my
clothes take off to clip a rose hey baby i killed this for you take
off my bomba when i samba through that front door deep in-
side i am a whore you can't call me a whore you can't ignore her
catholic sick her windswept mindset tombstone hairdo
rainforest shampoo any man will do when you have been alone
and don't know it your breast bone beats hard against your shirt
to cover up the hurt and how you suffer through supper its the
last time america's favorite pastime is to tell you how you stink
tell you how you think how you love how you know that fine
line from your tongue to the top of your crisscrossed head
means i sleep on dirty sheets sometimes i do cuz i'm alone i
sleep with my phone in one hand and my remote control in the
other so pissed at you blue lines lull a bye me to sleep and i
dream she comes to me in a tattered winter jacket black blond
dull eyes straight ahead melody something like doll parts some-
thing like touch me i'm sick scrawl across my mighty mouth i
was born in the south here i go i'm cajun again she speaks

french with a wrench in her teeth "voulez-vous couchez avec moi ce soir?" a rose is a rose is a rose is a fine white hair on a black shirt is a folded up number in the front of my african bag is a moment in time before a sidewalk warm tree fist fingernail silver ring chunk fist ring her toes point west and her chin lifts to the sun

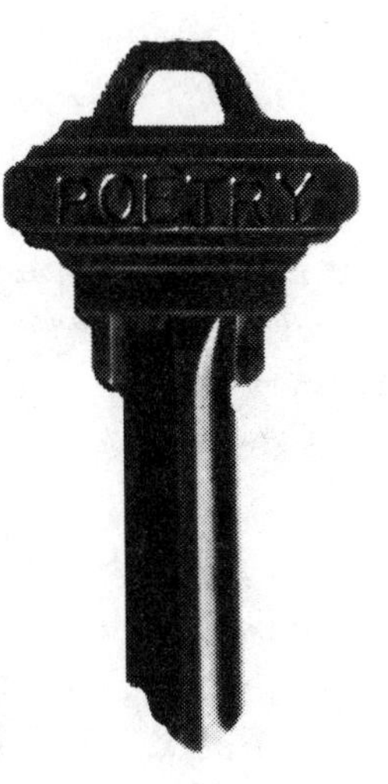
POETRY

reading list

Virginia Woolf, Naomi Wolf, Simone de Beauvoir, Susan Faludi, Beth Borrus, Lisa Campbell, *The Women's Encyclopedia of Myths and Secrets*, *The Encyclopedia of Amazons*, bell hooks, Rumi, Jenny Holzer, W. S. Burroughs, Eileen Myles, Gloria Steinem, *The New Censorship*, Hakim Bey, Jeanette Winterson, William Gibson, Emma Goldman, Michael Ondaatje, Anne Waldman, Bobbie Louise Hawkins, Zora Neale Hurston, *Caught Looking*, Harry Crews, Kathy Acker, *Lesbian Nuns: Breaking Silence*, Gertrude Stein, ntozake shange, Cookie Mueller, Mina Loy, *Inanna*, *Angry Women*, Ted Berrigan, John Weiners, Aime Cesaire, Apollinaire, Eloise Klein-Healy, Lucy Lippard, Toni Morrison, Judy Chicago, *Scum Manifesto*, Luisah Teish, H.D., Anna Akhmatova, Sappho, *Goddesses in Every Woman*, Bernadette Mayer...

listening list

Patti Smith, PJ Harvey, Michelle T. Clinton, Linda J. Albertano, the Stooges, the Babes, the Dicks, Bongwater, Carter Family, Woody Guthrie, Nico, Dvorak, MC Lyte, Daniel Johnston, Beck, the Last Poets, Thelonius Monk, Maggie Estep, Sonic Youth, mc 900 foot jesus, Bloodtest, Nirvana, Abra Joy Moore, Tommy Swerdlow, Janis Joplin, Merilene M. Murphy, Gram Parsons, Hank Williams, Irma Thomas, Bob Dylan, Gil Scott-Heron, Little Nicky Cave, WEBA, music of ancient Greece & Turkey, Disposable Heroes, Richard Thompson, Diamanda Galas, Lightnin' Hopkins, John Coltrane, Etta James, Velvets, Leadbelly, Nina Simone, Rosanne Cash, Sweet Honey in the Rock...

About the Author

Grew up in Texas, Louisiana Cajun by birth. Born May 21st, 1964. BA Humanities, UT Austin, concentration in writing/women's studies. First ever MFA class, Jack Kerouac School of Disembodied Poetics, the Naropa Institute in Boulder, Colorado; studied with the likes of Allen Ginsberg, Anne Waldman, Diane di Prima, Marianne Faithfull, Hakim Bey...among others. Performed and won awards nationally. Widely anthologized. Unrepentant Feminist. Activist by nature. Peer counselor, clinic defense, homeless writers, over a decade of femicentric art and politics. Ex-Catholic. Cajun/Latin/Moorish ancestor worship. Longtime involvement in indie music scene, got out before it was too late. Full length solo spoken word CD, *"Your Only Other Option Is Surgery"* out on New Alliance Records. Currently resides in Los Angeles, blazing into the future creating CD-ROM, technopoetics, writing for HBO, and cruising that *super* highway.